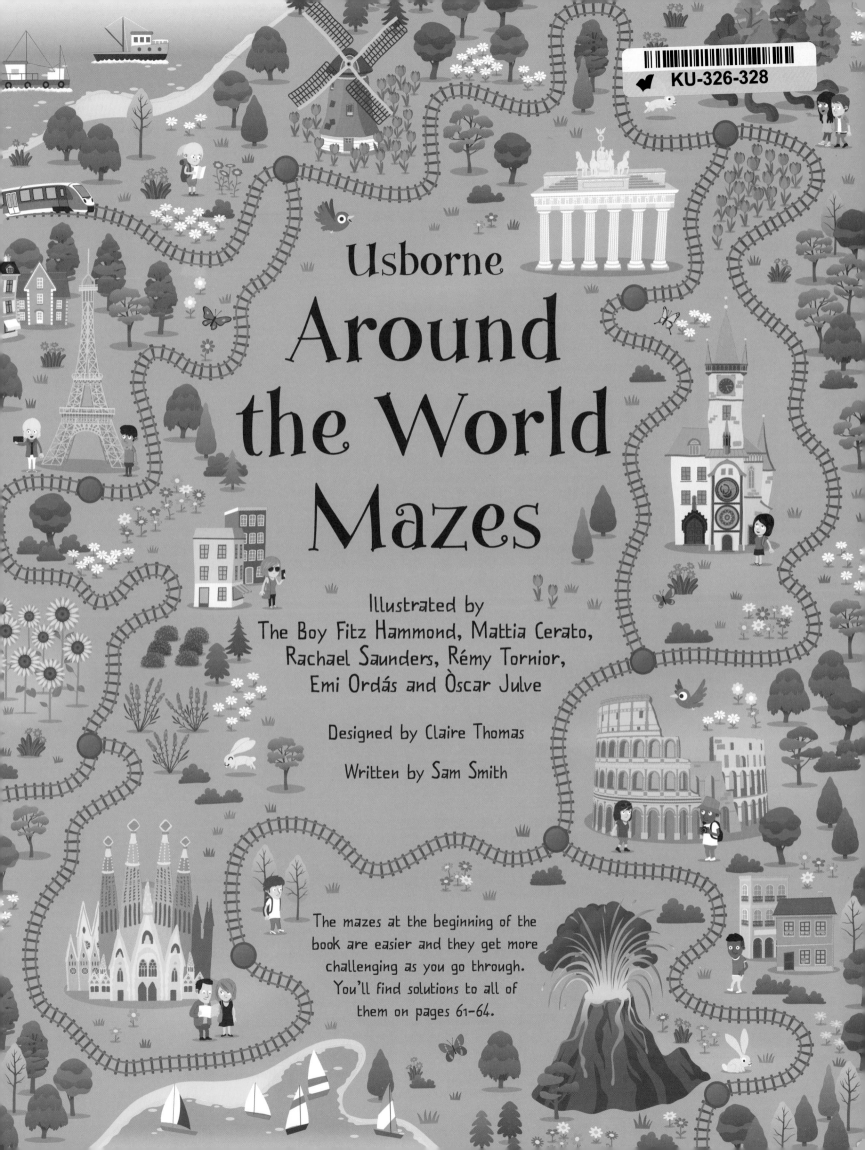

Usborne
Around the World Mazes

Illustrated by
The Boy Fitz Hammond, Mattia Cerato,
Rachael Saunders, Rémy Tornior,
Emi Ordás and Òscar Julve

Designed by Claire Thomas

Written by Sam Smith

The mazes at the beginning of the
book are easier and they get more
challenging as you go through.
You'll find solutions to all of
them on pages 61-64.

Venice visit

Seth wants a souvenir to take home from his visit to Venice. Guide him through the crowds in St. Mark's Square so he can select a Venetian mask from the stall.

River rafting

Help the team of rafters below the Victoria Falls Bridge battle the mighty Zambezi river and find their way to the finish, keeping to the foaming white-water paths.

START

FINISH

Route to the Rani Hotel

Guide Gopesh's tuk tuk along a clear path
through the bustling Indian market so he can
drop off his passenger outside the Rani Hotel.

Gopesh's
tuk tuk

5

Canoeing in Canada

Mia's supposed to be meeting her friends for a canoe trip around the Vancouver coast. Which way should she cycle through Stanley Park to reach them?

Mia

Mia's friends

Samba search

Gabriela is looking for Débora, her dancing partner, who's dressed in exactly the same outfit. Find where she is, then guide Gabriela to her through the Rio Carnival crowds.

Gabriela

8

Capital congestion

Steer Marco's moped through the gaps in the Paris traffic to join the other tourists admiring the Arc de Triomphe.

Marco

FINISH

Thai floating market

Nisa needs to paddle between the maze of boats to reach her friend waiting at the waterside. Which way should she go?

Nisa

FINISH

Nisa

Russian roads

Guide the yellow cab across Moscow to take its passengers to St. Basil's Cathedral, steering clear of any snowdrifts blocking the way.

St. Basil's
Cathedral

START

Surfing in the sun

The Hawaiian surf's up, and Will's ready to ride some waves. Find him a clear path from The Seaside Shack, across the busy beach, to the ocean.

FINISH

THE SEASIDE SHACK

Will

13

Barcelona blading

Help Roger rollerblade along the shortest route between the Barcelona buildings to visit the Sagrada Família church.

Sagrada Família

Roger

Arctic rescue

The polar ice is breaking apart! Guide the orange raft along a whale-free route to Base Camp, picking up all the researchers on the way, so they can retrieve their equipment.

START

BASE
CAMP

FINISH

Sailing in Sydney

Steer Stephen's boat to the jetty near the Sydney Opera House, keeping to the sailing routes shown.

FINISH

Stephen's boat

Egyptian excursion

Guide Ahmed and Kareem along the sandy paths to the pyramids, avoiding snakes and scorpions, and without passing any other camel riders.

FINISH

Ahmed and Kareem

A ramble in Rio

Callum climbed Corcovado mountain to see the Christ the Redeemer statue, but now he's feeling weary. He's staying at the yellow, beachside hotel – can you guide him along the trails and back between the buildings so he can relax in his room?

Callum

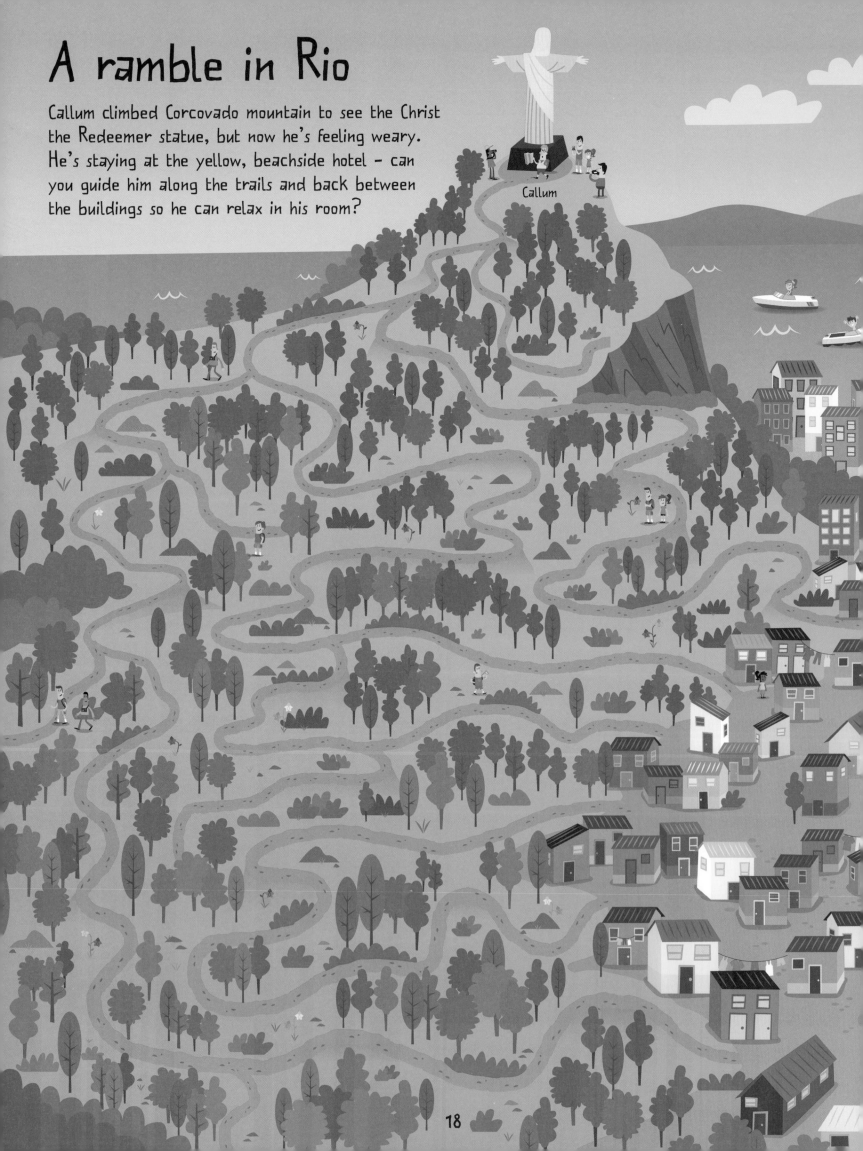

18

Safari snaps

Find a route for Guy and Greta to photograph the gorillas from all of the marked viewing points, then return to where they started, without taking any trail twice.

Viewing points look like this.

Guy and Greta

Old Town tour

Help Phoebe find her way through the Old Town in Dubrovnik to join the city wall tour that's about to begin.

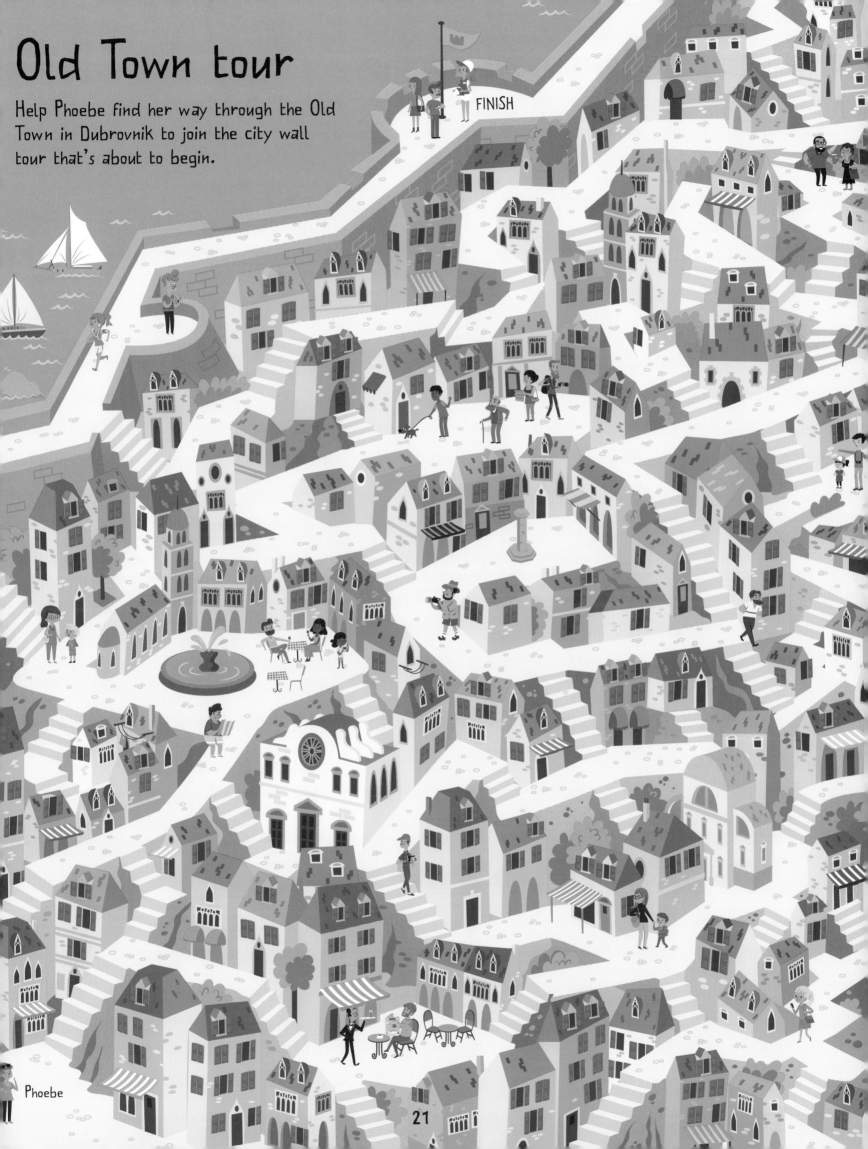

FINISH

Phoebe

Outback way back

Follow the footprints across the Australian outback to help Joey
return to his mother, without encountering any other kangaroos.

Joey

Joey's mother

23

Chinese panda park

Huan has just brought out a new basket of bamboo. Help Ping the panda reach the fresh food without bumping into any of his friends.

Ping

Huan

Night-ride in Norway

A group of guests is returning from a late-night husky ride under the Northern Lights. Can you lead their dogsled back along the lantern-lit trails to the ice hotel?

ICE HOTEL

START

25

Help the herd

The herd of gazelles needs to reach the watering hole for a drink, without passing any predators. Which way should they take along the African trails to avoid all the hungry hyenas and lurking lions?

Key:

Lion   Hyena

START

The watering hole

Tokyo crossing

Find a way through the Tokyo crowds for Saya so she can shop at the sales in the mall. She must keep to the crossings while walking over the roads.

Chinese lanterns

Guide Peijing back from the pagoda to the land, without pushing past any other people admiring the festival lanterns.

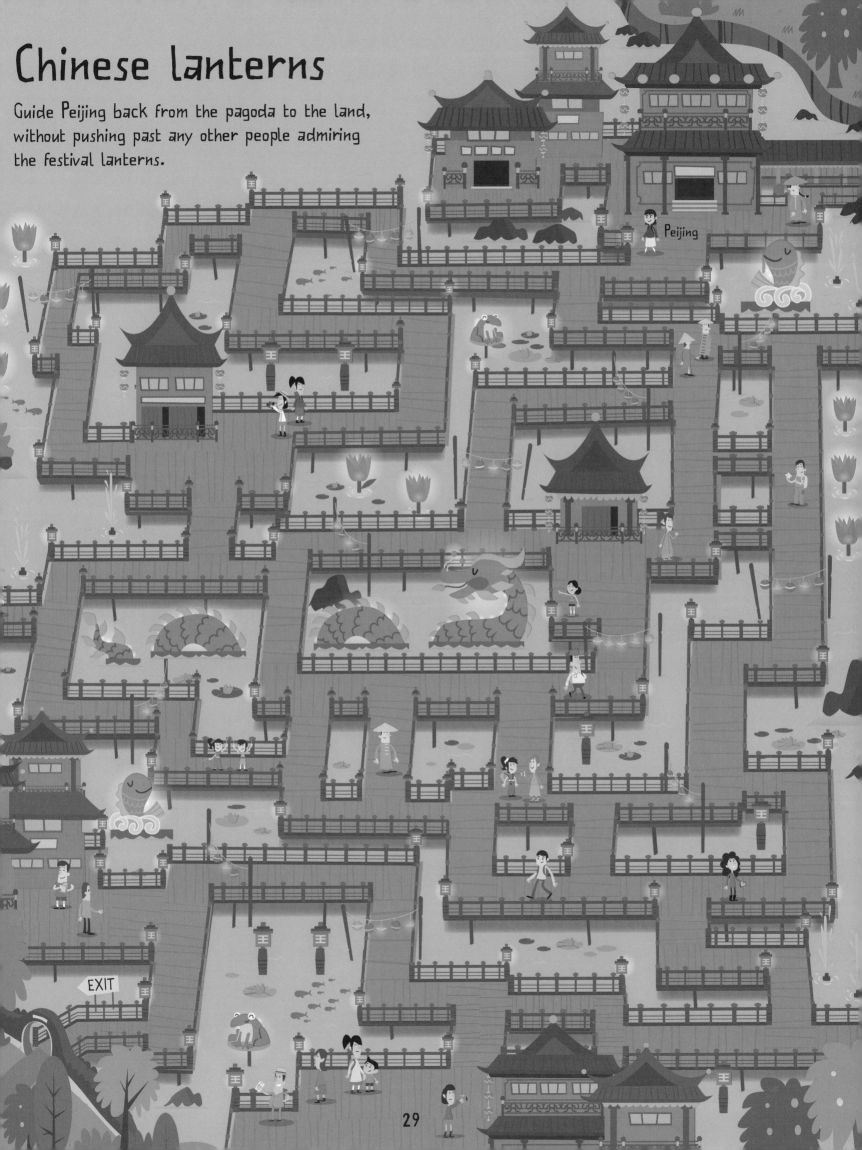

Peijing

EXIT

Everglade voyage

Find a path for Phil's airboat across the Florida swamp to the log cabin, without encountering any of the alligators lying in wait.

Phil

Athens Acropolis

Find Cressida a clear route across the Acropolis, between the rocks and ruins, so she can take a picture on the Parthenon steps.

The Parthenon

Cressida

Backpacking in Bavaria

Nina's hiking through the German hills to Neuschwanstein Castle. Which trails should she take to cross the bridge and find her way to the fairy-tale fortress?

Nina

TEGELBERG

NEUSCHWANSTEIN

Tour of the fjords

Steer the blue boat around these Norwegian sea inlets, landing at every wooden jetty on its way to Tromstad, without sailing any stretch of water twice.

START

Tromstad

35

Ranch round-up

The American cowboys are searching for some escaped cattle. Find Ralph a route along the trails to round up the five stray cows in this area, then lead them to the ranch, without going the same way twice.

RANCH

Ralph

Walk to the wall

The tour bus can't get any closer to the Great Wall of China. Help Heng guide the group to the stairs, so they can climb to the top of the wall. (They can walk past other people.)

Summer in Central Park

Kit's meeting some of his New York friends in Central Park for a kite-flying contest. Which route should he take to them so that he can buy a hot dog on his way, without needing to walk along any path twice?

Kit

Director's detour

Hollywood director Harvey is in a rush to reach Set 10, and doesn't want to be delayed. Find him a route so that he won't pass anyone walking along the roads.

Sowing seeds

Nengah needs to plant his rice in the last empty flooded field. Help him pick the quickest path to it down these Indonesian rice terraces, without pushing past any other workers.

Nengah

Hiking in the Himalayas

Guide the two hikers along the trails from their tent so they can reach the red flag and admire the mighty mountains around them. Where a trail ends, they must use the fixed ropes to climb up to a higher ledge.

START

Canyon crossing

Find Gary a clear route across the Arizona terrain to the Canyon Café. He mustn't enter the river, walk past red rockfall warning signs, or climb over any rocks in his way.

Gary

CANYON CAFÉ

European tour

Your train ticket can take you to each red stop just once. Plan a rail route to Pisa so you see all the named sights along the way.

START

Dutch Windmill

Brandenburg Gate

The Crooked Forest

Eiffel Tower

Prague Astronomical Clock

The Alps

Leaning Tower of Pisa

Sagrada Família church

Roman Colosseum

Mount Vesuvius

45

Amazon adventure

Seymour is searching for a red rainforest frog. Find one for him, then guide him to it along the river. If his way is blocked, he must find a gap to go ashore and carry his canoe between the bushes to rejoin the river elsewhere. (He can paddle both upstream and downstream.)

Seymour

London landmarks

Find the right route around London for the red tour bus. It must cross the river three times and finish at the London Eye, without taking any road twice.

START

49

London Eye

Yellowstone spring

Kev's camping in America's Yellowstone National Park, and wants to visit the Grand Prismatic Spring. Help him collect his eight friends from outside their tents, see the spring, and return to his tent without taking any trail twice.

Kev

GRAND PRISMATIC SPRING

Post at the Pole

Find a fish-free path between the rocks and penguins so Rhys and Rhonda can collect their mail from the South Pole post office.

Rhys and Rhonda

Andean expedition

Help the explorer pick out a path to the ancient Peruvian ruins on the other side of the valley, using the logs and rope bridges to cross the rivers and canyons.

Beautiful blossoms

Help Yukie and Hiro get a good look at all the Japanese cherry blossoms on their way to view Mount Fuji, without retracing their steps. The pink symbols on the paths show the best place to see each tree.

FINISH

Yukie and Hiro

Titicaca trip

Find the South American fisherman a route between the reeds and floating islands of Lake Titicaca to leave fish in each basket, without doubling back.

START

FINISH

Around the reef

Guide Alfie between the rocks and coral of this Australian reef, so he can snap all nine clownfish on his camera and finish back by the anchor. He doesn't want to swim any part of his route twice.

This is a clownfish.

FINISH

Alfie